CONTENTS

ACKNOWLEDGMENTS

Thank you to all the dedicated group members who submitted photos a second time around. Your pictures made the time spent putting this book together incredibly enjoyable.

Specifically: April Kolin for your "no school" picture, Elizabeth Gunnells for catching the pet store "experimenting" on the goldfish, Francisco Reyes for spotting the "stollen" dog, Jeremy J. Kruizenga for pointing out yet another Taco Bell Fail, Maritxu de Alaiza for the "RRZ RRZ RZZ," and Michael Kirchner for your many, many hilarious submissions. Even if I didn't mention you I thoroughly enjoyed looking through all of your pictures. Thank you for your services, as you courageously defended the Grammar Nation by keeping your cameras ready to shoot the grammatical offenders.

Thank you to my editor Daniela, who is always patient and helps me clarify my somewhat-spastic sense of humor into coherent writing. These books would not exist without you.

Thanks to my friends who have supported me during a very difficult year: Chandler Thomas, whose Twitter account never fails to entertain (and is always grammatically perfect); Elaine Savarese, whose Hall & Oates musical I dream about seeing; Joe Quinn, who selflessly gave me his room for the summer; Anna Zoeller, who will leave us to get her Ph.D. in English soon; Katie Abney, who I fully expect to see running a major magazine one day; Ryan Wilson, who will be walking me down the aisle at some point in the future (as a friend or as the groom has yet to be determined); Helen Van Wagoner, for whom I will gladly wear a purple bridesmaid dress; Chase Espy, who undoubtedly will be known as Judge Espy one day; Gloria Son, whose biting wit and feathered hair will always make me smile; Grace Nichols, my sister and best friend, for tagging me in your solo pics. Everyone else, you know who you are.

To my brother, who passed away this year, entirely too soon: I'm a better person because of the two months we had in Charleston. I love you, and I know that when you invented basketball you never dreamed it'd get this big.

To my sister and parents: Thank you, I love you, and it will get better.

One

BUSINESS AS USUAL

Alpine Sports now has two convenient locations for all your ski rental needs! Our newest location is in the Parkway Plaza just steps for City Liquors and City Market! And we still offer a Ski Rental Shuttle directly to your holiday home. We will pick you up and take you to Alpine Sports and deliver you back to your door. If you are in need of accessories and ski clothing, we have a huge selection to choose from.

Two locations conveniently located at the intersection of Main St. & Ridge St., and in the Parkway Shopping Plaza with plenty of parking available.

70.453.8100

It's understandable to get "form" and "from" mixed up, but substituting "for" is borderline ridiculous.

(2)

"Tetanus" must have that "a" in the middle. Otherwise — combined with the electronic lights — this sign is reminiscent of Tetris, the admittedly awesome video game.

**If your paying
too much for you're
Spring Shopping**

Cut It Out

Fairfax Corner

Whoever made this sign should cut it out, e.g., cut out two words and switch them.

(4)

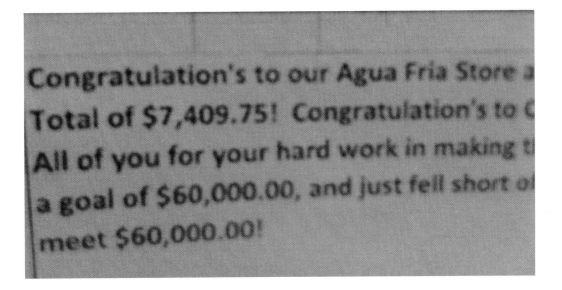

Congratulation's to our Agua Fria Store a
Total of $7,409.75! Congratulation's to C
All of you for your hard work in making t
a goal of $60,000.00, and just fell short o
meet $60,000.00!

Congratulations on [not] understanding the possessive form.

Please don't. You clearly have other things to worry about.

The creator of this sign needs a remedial sixth-grade English course.

We're not aware of "his'n" ever being acceptable, even in the coarsest slang.

Gangsters should know how to spell. Otherwise they are much less intimidating.

If you bought either of these shirts, do the world a favor and don't get any more tattoos. And please don't have any more children.

THE WORLDS ONLY PROTECTIVE SHEET

Q: WHATS THE DIFFERENCE BETWEEN A FLY SHEET & A PROTECTIVE SHEET?

A: PIECE OF MIND.

FIND U

WWW.KENSINGTONPRODUCTS.COM

This poor animal is wearing a picnic tablecloth in a horribly written ad.
It's probably better that its eyes are covered.

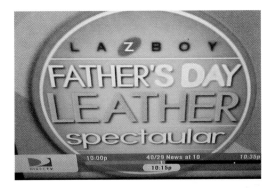

The world would be a better place if TVs had spell check.

Doesn't experimenting on animals usually take place in labs, not pet stores?

Salon & Café

$40 HAIR CUTS
TUESDAY'S & WEDNESDAY'S

Something that appears twice in this banner needs to be cut.

At least this person was consistently wrong.

(12)

S & J Carpentry Ltd

Exhibition's
Display's
Bespoke unit's
Shopfitting

Tel: 01375 893 864

Fax: 01375 893812

The service at this establishment is clearly superior. You don't even have to wash your own hands.

Isn't there spell check on the software used to make banners? Or common sense in the people who make them?

You'd think if a person can spell "affordability" correctly they'd know the difference between "its" and "it's."

"Wardreobe." That's a fun new word.

Please refrain from using unnecessary apostrophes. Thanks.

Two
∧

STATE LAW STOP
WHILE BUS IS

LOADING AND UNLOADING

There should be a state law forbidding misspelled words on government property.

Maybe they should rethink canceling school that day.

This doesn't bode well for the future of Texas education.

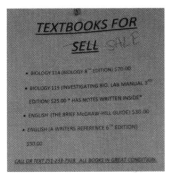

One of those textbooks probably shows the difference between the words "sell" and "sale." Maybe instead of selling them, you should reread them.

Dear Lord, please don't let this man get elected.

This must be an incredibly small school.

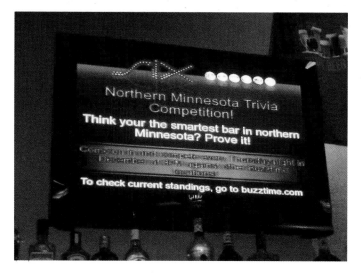

Do we really need to prove it?

Poor public-speaking class. It must have cankles.

Instead of a student union for hanging out, this school should have more classrooms. You know, for learning.

This might be excusable—if an elementary school student put it up. Somehow we doubt that was what happened.

Three

^

TALKING OBJECTS

Are the contents of this box something else pretending to be a shelf?

The bald eagle soaring over the snow-capped mountains says "thank you" to the nurses and staff of St. Charles Hospital. Why? Only he knows.

What did you do to alarm the door? And why would you want to upset it?

THIS DOOR IS NOW
ALARMED

Use only in the case of an *emergency.*

This pamphlet is practically on its knees begging you to answer its question. It is apparently speaking.

There are several possibilities here:

- The sign is using quotation marks ironically, so it's actually not sorry that no pets are allowed. It hates animals, anyway.
- The sign itself is embarrassed that somebody forced it to display the rule against pets, so it's apologizing to potentially upset petlovers. If the sign had its way, pets would be welcome.
- The sign creator doesn't know what quotation marks mean.

Ironic quotation marks or fake computers?

Four
∧
HIGH TECH

clockDSCN5304BW.jpg

clockDSCN5305BW.jpg

Files

cloc

cloc

Import to internal memory? If the same file has already been added, the file is overwrited.

ot

96.

cloc

cloc

cloc

| Yes | No |

cloc

clockDSCN5305BW.jpg
11/Feb/2010   3.281 MB
3648x2736

Something in this picture needs to be overwrited.

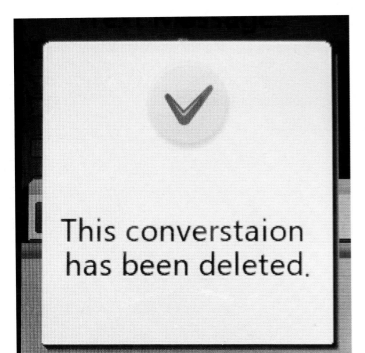

This is almost another new word: converstaion.

8. ENGINEER (v1.1)
★★★★ by SAMGLONICJON2791 on Oct...
Program is practically useless.

9. Too basic (v1.1)
★★ by Claudia Samaniego on Sep 12,...
Hi! Already bought this app. I'm ESL student, but it is to basic for me, I was thinking that this app. Could help me to understand how to write in advanced grammar, but no! It's to simple and basic it's better a dictionary!

10. Needs Examples (v1.1)
★★★★ by jhitch on Sep 11, 2009
It would be nice to see some examples of proper usage under punctation etc.

More Reviews...

These are the reviews from a grammar iPhone application (which we won't name).

Commas and apostrophes are *not* interchange-able, and even if they were this would still be incorrect.

Leather Couch with Automen -- Great condition - $585 (Leucadia Encinitas)

Date: 2011-04-13, 8:45PM PDT

Reply to: [Errors when replying to ads?]

Brand new 5 years ago $2150 and rarely used as it was in living room and we always hung out in the family room!

does not have recliners, its a 4 piece sectional with each unit with a slight angle so as it fits together creates a arc as seen in the second picture

Selling because moving.

- Location: Leucadia Encinitas
- it's NOT ok to contact this poster with services or other commercial interests

http://sandiego.craigslist.org/ssd/fuo/2324056464.html

The lack of intelligible copy on this ad is almost as impressive as the "automen" in

the posting's title. Quick! Free-associate: Automen. Ottoman. Automatic ottoman?

(37)

THANK YOU FOR YOUR INTEREST IN VERZION WIRELESS.

We have a sneaking suspicion that whoever created this ad was fired. They spelled the name of the company wrong.

Verizon Wireless offers a large selection of the latest phones. Here are some recommendations to help you pick out the perfect one for your needs.

Continue Shopping

Haven't quite found what you are looking for?

All Phones ›
Smartphones ›
Internet Devices ›
Accessories ›

Samsung Fascinate
★★★★½
(read 421 reviews)* *

2-yr Contract Price	$299.99
Online Discount	-$100.00
Your Price	$199.99*

Other Popular Devices

Motorola DROID 2
★★★★★
(read 768 reviews)*

2-yr Contract Price	$299.99
Online Discount	-$100.00
Your Price	$199.99*

HTC DROID INCREDIBLE
★★★★★
(read 3,024 reviews)*

2-yr Contract Price	$299.99
Online Discount	-$100.00
Your Price	$199.99*

BlackBerry Bold 9650 smartphone
★★★★½
(read 548 reviews)*

2-yr Contract Price	$249.99
Online Discount	-$100.00
Your Price	$149.99*

* Based on customer reviews as of 10/26/2010. New 2-YR renewal req'd. 3G multimedia phones require voice plan with data pack $9.99 or higher. 3G Smartphones require voice plan with data pack

Five
∧
QUESTIONABLE INTENTIONS

This penny-smashing machine has something in common with many, many Americans right now.

From what we can tell, the bottom line was supposed to say "we sale Sunday bear." Oh, okay.

This company might brew excellence only during the last weekend of July or only during the last week at the end of July. Although either interpretation doesn't make much sense. (41)

It's a good guess to say that this was intentional.

The more important question: Why?

The two possible interpretations of this are pretty obvious. Either way, we will not be visiting this establishment.

Clearly unintentional, and oddly sweet.

Ah, witty replies to bathroom

graffiti always make us smile.

The intended verb in the second line of the de-

scription gives us pause.

The unintentionally ironic quotation marks strike

again.

Claiming you're perfect is a dangerous game.

We'd like to meet this guy named Wing.

This is a Self Clearing Restaurant.

Please take your tray to the trolleys provided.

Thank you.

My, my, technology certainly has become advanced.

Honk if you're judging this guy!

We're pretty sure badass ladies also know how to spell "bad."

Do the bras own the ladies?

What's the landlord wanted for? And should he be dead or alive?

The door is also a lock? Are doors and locks the same thing now?

Six

∧

TRANSPORTATION, TRAVEL, & LEISURE

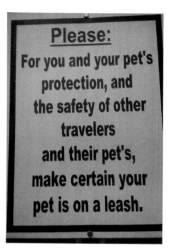

Please:
For you and your pet's
protection, and
the safety of other
travelers
and their pet's,
make certain your
pet is on a leash.

Two different uses of "pet," yet consistent apostrophe use. One of these is wrong.

For your protection
Any person who assaults a passenger or employe of CTA
can, under the law, be imprisoned
for up to ten years!

Para su proteccion
¡Cualquier persona que asalte a un pasajero o empleado del CTA puede,
bajo la ley, ser puesta en prision por un termino hasta de diez años!

Chicago Transit Authority

We'd argue that the person who created this sign deserves jail time.

How many violators?

Apparently many people don't know how to make a word possessive.

93st Annual Cherry Festival

CITIZEN OF THE YEAR

DONNA FRANCO

Imagining how one would pronounce "93st" is highly amusing.

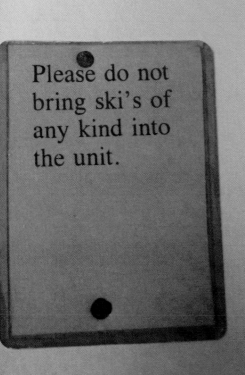

Please do not bring ski's of any kind into the unit.

The possessive strikes again. We wonder if this is the most confusing part of the English language for native speakers.

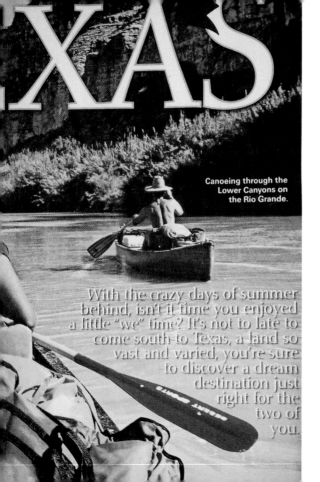

Canoeing through the Lower Canyons on the Rio Grande.

With the crazy days of summer behind, isn't it time you enjoyed a little "we" time? It's not to late to come south to Texas, a land so vast and varied, you're sure to discover a dream destination just right for the two of you.

When the purpose of your business is to publish written works, you should probably have the "to"/"too"/"two" distinction down pat.

LOCAL AREA INFORMATION

Local Hotel's

There are numerous Hotels' of all types within 30 minutes of Lackland AFB. Those mentioned herein are listed due to their convenient proximity to the base. This is not an endorsement of their products.

This person tried it two different ways in this ad and neither succeeded. Maybe the third time's the charm.

This person misspelled "vacuum." But far more troubling is the fact that there's a vacuum by this free-standing jail cell. We won't even ask why.

This could be your tax dollars at work, folks.

This would be funnier if it were "parks and recreatoin."

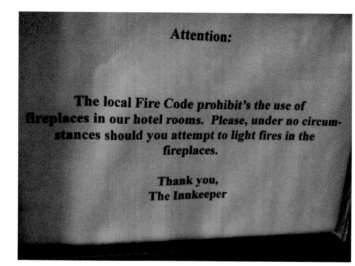

Attention:

The local Fire Code prohibit's the use of fireplaces in our hotel rooms. Please, under no circumstances should you attempt to light fires in the fireplaces.

**Thank you,
The Innkeeper**

Who cares about incorrect possessives? Just DO NOT, UNDER ANY CIRCUMSTANCES, light a fire in your fireplace.

This sign was created in response to the great paring epidemic of 2010.

This guy gets extra points for the "Khan" pun, which are immediately cancelled out by the missing apostrophe in "cant."

A rolling stone gathers no

moss.

That's an inventive use of the

number 1. May we buy a real

vowel, please?

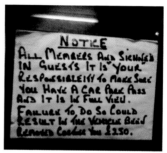

Sports team allegiances are hardcore. Apparently hatred of one's rival can cause brain cramps, shortness of breath, and blindness.

It is "your" responsibility. And we applaud "your" failed effort of creating a noun by adding "ity" to "resposible."

After reading this we can't help imagining 100 human "feets" lined up as a measuring tool.

Let's blame this one on the alcohol.

Take a hike. No, seriously.

Seven
^

REALLY? REALLY.

Redundancy anyone, anyone?

But wait… isn't smoking bad for you?

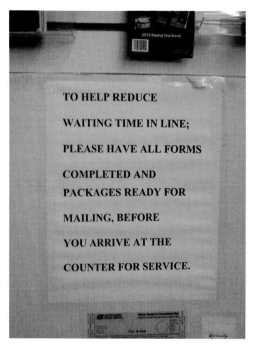

TO HELP REDUCE

WAITING TIME IN LINE;

PLEASE HAVE ALL FORMS

COMPLETED AND
PACKAGES READY FOR

MAILING, BEFORE

YOU ARRIVE AT THE

COUNTER FOR SERVICE.

Unnecessary punctuation probably hurts your eyes as much as it does ours.

IBAR
CORRECT THE FOLLOWING ERRORS
BEFORE RELEASING THIS IBAR

PIECE COUNT MUST BE GREAT THAN 0.

They were on the right track here…

NOTICE

FILL TANK SLOW

This sign illustrates another problem America is facing: the disappearance of the adverb. Please, do your part to save the adverbs.

(71)

We think the dog ran away on its own.

M. Smith Carpets

This Prosses is to be seen to believed !!!

Introducing a new revolutionary
process of carpet cleaning
suitable for all types
of dwellings.
U doen dit met u beste klere . . .
Laat ons u matte ook
droogskoonmaak
Ons maak geen geraas so kan
die werk voortgaan terwyl ons werk.

Contact us for a free and hightly
competitive QUOTATION
* * *
Martin   Elsa
084-655-6018   073 0377 698

This flyer looks like the result of putting text into a cheap online translator then mixing it with a four-year-old's spelling.

It appears Flava-Flav has gone green. He's sponsoring his own vegetables now.

Aside from the unnecessary apostrophe, this sign at a chiropractor's office is probably not politically correct.

Okay, maybe they ran out of room on the first line. But wow, that's an expensive chicken tender meal. And they also ran out of "o"s?

What is a "beverage tapper container"?

CARE INSTRUCTIONS FOR ICE TEA
BEVERAGE TAPPER CONTAINER

Prior to using this product, you should wash it in warm soapy water, using a mild detergent. When the plastic lid is firmly secured, you may pour directly from the container by flipping the lid vent open. inside nut in a clockwise rotation, Press, and release the spigot plunger to assure its Be sure to tighten the spigot by hand turning the proper positioning. **Caution: Never pour boiling or extremely hot liquid into the container, and never place the container over an open fire, or other heating element. In addition, never use this product in a microwave oven.**

For general cleaning, remove the plunger, and rinse with clean water, Do not remove the spigot, or rubber gasket encircling the hole,Do not use a scouring pad on the glass suface, Use only a sponge and mild detergent.**Caution: Never use this product in a dish washer**

When using this product to prepare ice tea, always be sure the lid is securely tightened before lifting witn lid handle. Occasionally, heat fron the sun can loosen the lid. Always hold the jar with both hands when lifting, and never lift with the handle alone. To prevent scratching, use only non-metallic utensils in the glass jar.

This beverage container is made of top - quality materials, and is designed for your convenience, We hope that you will enjoy using your beverage tapper container.

Perhaps this is forgivable because it was made by a young Girl Scout troop. But where were their parents?

This banner illustrates why you should always carry a Sharpie. It's deserving of some guerilla justice, grammar Nazi-style.

Where have all the adverbs gone?

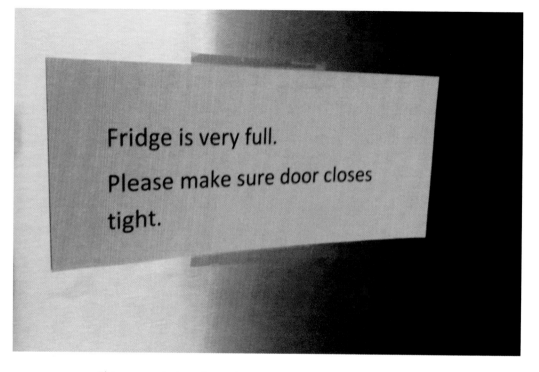

Fridge is very full.

Please make sure door closes tight.

There seems to be a theme here.

TO OUR VALUED CUSTOMERS

One of our escalators are out of order, still waiting for the special part to fix, Please walk or use the elevator when needed. Sorry for any inconvenience it may have cause.

At least this sign is very polite, if very ungrammatical.

A Google search of the word "aprons" reveals that this misspelling is apparently a common mistake. How disheartening.

Subway Management

SNEEZ GARD

(a thing to block your sneez from getting to the food)

Oh! That's what a sneez gard is.

The early bird should use her extra time to study grammar.

I wish that you could spell.

For the children's edification, please use proper punctuation.

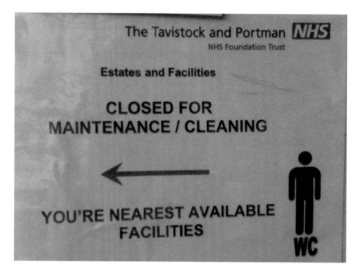

You are nearest available facilities. Oh, thanks.

This had to be on purpose, right? Or maybe the stencilbearer is Russian.

Eight

IN OTHER NEWS...

He's seen the future and it holds many wars.

You're making our eyes hurt.

Bad grammar at its most widely visible.

"Legisil" is a new cream for something conta-gious. This square is sponsored by its creators.

THE SHEEN INTERVIEW
EXCLUSIVE: SHEEN TO SUE CBS
"THERE GONNA LOSE IN A COURT"

If they don't even know the "there"/"they're"/"their" distinction, they probably are going to lose in court.

Where the News Comes First

ARE THEIR MORE VICTIMS?

Yes. Every viewer who saw this.

The president had already been elected when this aired, so spelling his name wrong is pretty inexcusable. Ditto mistaking "formally" for "formerly."

Nine

WORD OF MOUTH

START OFF RIGHT WITH ONE OR TWO OF THESE DELICIOUS APPETIZERS:

Onion Rings • *NEW* Clamstrips • Kettle-Cooked Chips

Fresh-Fried Jalapeño Coins • Cheese Sticks
NEW Zucchini • *NEW* Mushrooms

SINGLE ORDER - 2.99
DOUBLE COMBO - Pick any two - 5.79
Served with ranch, marinara, Thai Chili Sauce, Campfire Sauce or tarter sauce

Would anyone like some tarter sauce with your jalapeño coins?

WE ARE OUT OF SPINACH UNTILL MONDAY
SORRY THE INCONVIENCE

Let's hope the spinach comes in by Monday, otherwise innocent customers will be subjected to this sign far longer.

Greek Omelette
Bacon Cheese omelette $7.99
Mushroom Cheese omelette $7.99
Spinach cheese omelette $7.99
Western Cheese omelette $8.99
Pepper Onion omelette $7.99
American cheese Omelette $6.99
Swiss cheese Omelette $6.99
Breakfast Wrap $7.99
Plain Omelette $5.99

All above served with Coffee Home Fries
and Toast. White eggs extra $1.00

Fried Cod
Chips $

All the abc
with fre
pickle,
fish
served w

"Coffee home fries" sounds like a kooky gourmet dish made by a bored chef. And brown eggs are less expensive than white ones.

ALL NESTLE COOKIE
PRODUCTS ARE
TEMPORARY OUT
OF STOCK

This appears to be at least an attempt at using an adverb, though it landed way off the mark.

The King of the Jungle on sale here 24 hours a day. Also, make sure you get your daily serving of vegetabels.

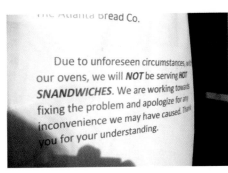

You'll probably never again see a sandwich so epically butchered.

The lemon shake-ups only have $1.50. Could you spare some change?

Thurs, Fri, Sat Starting at 1am.

Mon thru Sun, Best happy hour
$1.25 drafts, $6.00 Pitchers, $3.

Sunday $2 mimosas, screwdrive
$10 bottle of Champaign with a c

The Yankees would save a ton of money if they knew about these $6 pitchers. More important, though, is "champaign" a cross between a drink and a political candidate's efforts to get elected?

Billard: A duck that likes to play pool? A biller who's also a bastard? Sure.

Whoever wrote the contents of this fortune cookie did not foresee their mistake being captured on film and widely distributed.

There are no words. No really, one of these is not a real word.

If you never had any doubts about Taco Bell before, this should do it.

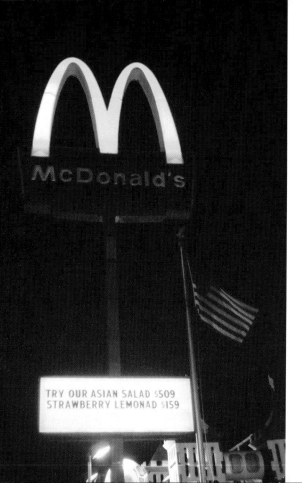

This could be correct. If all words were spelled phonetically.

If you're charging $159 for lemonade, you could at least afford to buy a vowel.

Oh good, the breakfast bur-
ritos got their coffee.

Although the food is Mexican, we're pretty sure the masterminds behind Chipotle speak English as a first language.

A less charitable reader would think this label refers to something scandalous.

(102)

Once again, attack of the phonetic spellers!

Does this mean crumbled AND creamed? Interesting.

Since everybody knows what a "combo" is, perhaps the sign writer should have relied on that handy abbreviation. It's easier to get right.

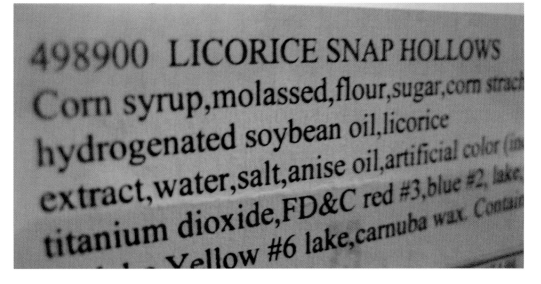

498900 LICORICE SNAP HOLLOWS
Corn syrup,molassed,flour,sugar,corn starch
hydrogenated soybean oil,licorice
extract,water,salt,anise oil,artificial color (in
titanium dioxide,FD&C red #3,blue #2, lake,
Yellow #6 lake,carnuba wax. Contain

Oh, snap! Your licorice just got molassed.

Unnecessary apostrophes strike again! It seems they're multiplying.

Somebody was drinking and making signs.

IF YOUR DRINKING
TO FORGET...
PLEASE PAY IN
ADVANCE.

Thanks. Management

Chockolate milk: chock full o' chocolate.

HILL COUNTRY RV RESORT

SODA/WATER/TEA PRICES

SODA	$ 1.00
WATER	$ 1.25
TEA	$ 1.25
MONSTER	$ 2.25
RED BULL	$ 2.50
CHOCKOLATE MILK	$ 2.25
JUICES	$ 2.25
½ PINK WHILE MILK	$ 1.25

(107)

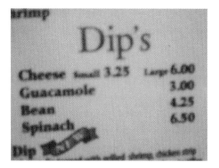

This dip owns cheese, guacamole, spinach, and a single bean. How lovely.

I'm afraid it's only infatuation. But how flattering.

Rise and shine! Use proper spelling!

Purshasing too many drinks may lead to slurred spelling.

Breakfast *JOEL'S* Resaurant
& Deli

The correct possessive apostrophe is exciting but immediately canceled out by the misspelled "restaurant."

Ten
^

DIRE WARNINGS

To all cashier / cooks i don't know who you are but if i find out you will be suspended for the first time and the second time you will be fired,if you are caught.When we get ice we do not put the bucket inside of the machine use the scoope

please.

Anything menacing about this warning is entirely diminished by the second-grade spelling and punctuation. When we get ice, we use the scoope. Duh.

NEED A PASSPORT! APPLICATIONS ACCEPTED IN PERSONNEL OFFICE!

The arbitrary capitalization and punctuation in this sign make it come off like a demand. Get a passport…or else.

It's too bad that not knowing how to spell "disturb" undermines any authority communicated by the skull and crossbones. It's kind of like seeing a police officer driving a Segway.

Your British neighbors are trying to be civilised this time. Don't make them get the hose.

Could they have meant "quite pleasing"?

Maybe "unattendent" means "with a terrible attendant."—like an infant or a drunken teenager or a DMV worker.

Maybe the author of this sign forgot a word at the end. "Stinger" would work.

When readers inevitably get angry at the lack of punctuation in this sign, its creator is responsible for subsequent damage.

You guys should reading the rules and regulation for parking in the community (5) Days And 5day only can you PARK IN the visitors space your Red Honda Civic has to be move even if its to the next space, Pictures has to been taken AND space marked by towed company

"Pictures has to been taken and space marked by towed company." Got that? Good.

Quite please? Oh, quite thank you.

No, you are on camera.

PHOTO CREDITS

Rowena Aburto: 82 (left); Victoria Barranco: 90; Joshua Bertram: 44 (left), 100 (right); Ryan Billings: 107 (top); Patti Bondurant: 37, 38; Katharine Boyle: 13, 100 (left), 101; Mike Brabham: 109 (bottom); Elaine Braun-Keller: 21 (bottom right); Natalie Burke: 16 (bottom); Bri Catarino: 95 (bottom); Laura Chandler: 22 (top), 36 (right), 87 (bottom); David Chesler: 71; Joshua Christensen: 49; Amy Clawson Stier: 40 (top), 69, 93, 112 (bottom); Joe Collins: 99 (bottom left); Jolyn Curfman: 77, 86 (bottom); Siobhan Currell: 23 (top right), 47 (right), 50 (left), 61, 82 (right), 83, 84 (top), 108 (bottom); Ward Davis: 48 (left), 65, 66, 110; Maritxu de Alaiza: 103; Andrea Derrick: 3, 40 (bottom); Michael Douglas: 31, 57, 81 (top), 115; Andrea Dragna: 52 (top), 86 (top), 112 (top), 113 (top); Sarah Flory: 60 (bottom), 117 (left); Nathan Frandino: 106; Philip Gallegos: 116; Parks Gilbert: 59 (bottom); Abigail Grant: 67; Vikky Grey: 64 (middle); Elizabeth Gunnells: 11 (right); Amy Harshman: 94 (top); Tylene Headley: 23; Edward Jablonski: 27; Michael Kirchner: 15, 16 (top), 30, 45, 46, 58, 59 (top), 88, 89, 104 (bottom), 105; April Kolin: 20 (right), 52 (bottom); Jordana Lorraine Kotlus: 12, 43 (right); Jeremy J. Kruizenga: 75, 99 (bottom right); Jeanne LaSala: 43 (left); Annelies Lindemans: 4; Gemma Marshall: 73, 113 (bottom); Bill Mattinson: 95 (top); Brian McGarry: 7 (bottom); Celeste McCabe: 8, 9; Mac McCabe: 36 (left), 54, 78; Laurie Nash: 102 (right); Randy Neal: 107 (bottom); Tanay Nestico: 48 (right), 62, 63, 64 (top), 84 (bottom); Grace Nichols: 21 (bottom left); Sharon Nichols: 17, 47 (left), 50 (right), 108 (top); Katie Noles: 102 (left); Kaylee Nonnemacher: 44 (right), 78 (top); Lisa Nordyke: 114 (bottom); Nicole Pace: 81 (bottom right); Nicole Page: 23 (top left); David Parette: 10, 97; Jessica Pellman: 76; Tom Phillipson: 117 (right); Daniela Rapp: 14, 74, 81 (bottom left), 87 (top), 109 (top); Meigan Rath: 22 (bottom), 55, 56, 79, 80; Hilary Ray: 98; Francisco Reyes: 72; Brian Reynolds: 20 (left), 21 (top); Maria Photopulos: 29; Ashley Rooks: 5, 41, 53 (top), 70, 94 (bottom); Deanne Rowe: 11 (left); Gabriella Russotti: 28, 42; Peter Scoblic: 60 (top); Darren Spain: 96; Chandler Thomas: 26; Alaina Thonsgaard: 2, 34, 68, 92; Jenn Trommelen-Jones: 35; Holly Whitley: 53 (bottom), 99 (top), 114 (top); Martin Windolf: 104 (top)

Still not enough bad grammar, hair-raising spelling errors, and laugh-out-loud linguistic slipups?

See how many mistakes you can find in...

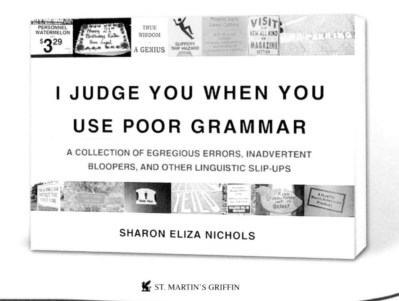

I JUDGE YOU WHEN YOU

USE POOR GRAMMAR

A COLLECTION OF EGREGIOUS ERRORS, INADVERTENT
BLOOPERS, AND OTHER LINGUISTIC SLIP-UPS

SHARON ELIZA NICHOLS

ST. MARTIN'S GRIFFIN